Test Book

Multiple-choice Tests
Short-answer Tests

Great Source Education Group

a Houghton Mifflin Company

Wilmington, Massachusetts

www.greatsource.com

AUTHORS

Laura Robb
Author

Powhatan School, Boyce, Virginia
Laura Robb, author of *Teaching Reading in Middle School, Teaching Reading in Social Studies, Science, and Math, Redefining Staff Development,* and *Literacy Links*, has taught language arts at Powhatan School in Boyce, Virginia, for more than 35 years. She is a co-author of the *Reader's Handbooks* for grades 4–5 and 6–8, as well as the *Reading and Writing Sourcebooks* for grades 3–5 and the *Summer Success: Reading Program*. Robb also mentors and coaches teachers in Virginia public schools and speaks at conferences throughout the country.

April Nauman
Contributing Author

Northeastern Illinois University, Chicago, Illinois
April D. Nauman, Ph.D., is a teacher educator at Northeastern Illinois University in Chicago. For more than 10 years she has worked with Chicago area elementary and high school teachers to improve literacy instruction for their students, mostly in high-needs city schools. Dr. Nauman has authored many papers on literacy learning.

Donna Ogle
Contributing Author

National-Louis University, Evanston, Illinois
Donna M. Ogle, Professor of Reading and Language at National-Louis University in Evanston, Illinois, served as President of the International Reading Association 2001–2002. Her extensive staff development experiences include working in Russia and other eastern European countries as part of the Reading and Writing for Critical Thinking Project from 1999–2003. Her latest books are *Coming Together as Readers* (2001, Skylight Professional Books) and *Reading Comprehension: Strategies for Independent Learners*, co-authored with Camille Blachowicz (Guilford, 2000). She is also a senior consultant for McDougal Littell's history text, *Creating America* (2000).

Editorial: Developed by Nieman Inc. with Phil LaLeike

Design: Ronan Design: Sean O'Neill

Illustrations: Mike McConnell

Printed in the United States of America
International Standard Book Number: 0-669-51429-2
1 2 3 4 5 6 7 8 9—QW—10 09 08 07 06 05 04

Table of Contents

3

Introduction to the *Test Book*

The *Test Book* includes short-answer tests and multiple-choice tests for each lesson in the *Reader's Handbook*. The test questions are based on the Quick Assess checklists found in the *Teacher's Guide and Lesson Plans Book*.

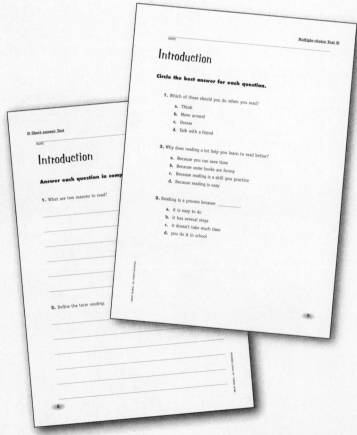

Use the tests as formal tools to assess students' understanding of the reading strategies and tools presented in the handbook.

Additional Assessment Tools

The *Reader's Handbook* program contains additional assessment tools in the *Teacher's Guide and Lesson Plans* book. Each lesson in the *Teacher's Guide and Lesson Plans* ends with two pages that offer ways to assess students' understanding of the lesson.

Use the Quick Assess checklist to determine whether students should work on the material either a) with guided practice or b) independently.

Guided Practice

Use the *Student Applications Book* pages for each lesson to work in small groups with students who need extra help.

Independent Practice

Students who have a grasp of the concepts in the lesson can do the activities described in this section.

Assessment Rubrics

Use these rubrics, located in the *Test Book*, to take a quick informal assessment of each student.

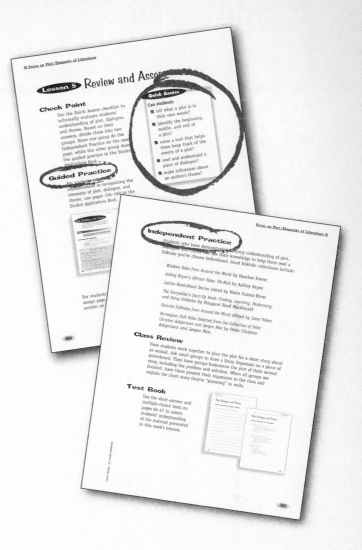

NAME

Introduction

Answer each question in complete sentences.

1. What are two reasons to read?

....

....

....

....

....

2. Define the term *reading*.

....

....

....

....

....

NAME ....

Introduction

Circle the best answer for each question.

1. Which of these should you do when you read?

    a. Think

    b. Move around

    c. Dream

    d. Talk with a friend

2. Why does reading a lot help you learn to read better?

    a. Because you can save time

    b. Because some books are funny

    c. Because reading is a skill you practice

    d. Because reading is easy

3. Reading is a process because _____.

    a. it is easy to do

    b. it has several steps

    c. it doesn't take much time

    d. you do it in school

NAME

The Reading Process—Before Reading

Answer each question in complete sentences.

1. Why do you set a reading purpose?

....

....

....

....

....

....

2. What are two things to look for when you preview a reading?

....

....

....

....

....

....

NAME ....

The Reading Process—Before Reading

Circle the best answer for each question.

1. What does a reading purpose tell?

    a. The number of pages

    b. The author's name

    c. What you want to find out from reading

    d. The most important idea

2. What should you look for when you preview a story?

    a. The title

    b. The first sentence

    c. Any pictures

    d. All of the above

3. What do you do when you make a reading plan?

    a. Choose a reading strategy.

    b. Talk with a friend.

    c. Look at the front and back cover.

    d. Guess how long it will take you to read.

NAME ....

The Reading Process—During Reading

Answer each question in complete sentences.

1. What question should you ask when you read with a purpose?

....

....

....

....

....

2. How do you connect to what you are reading?

....

....

....

....

....

The Reading Process—During Reading

Circle the best answer for each question.

1. Which step is part of the During Reading stage?

    a. Plan

    b. Preview

    c. Connect

    d. Set a Purpose

2. What do active readers do during reading?

    a. They visualize.

    b. They make predictions.

    c. They take notes.

    d. All of the above

3. When you connect to what you are reading, you _____.

    a. relate it to your own life

    b. find out about the author's life

    c. underline the main idea

    d. read parts of it aloud

NAME

The Reading Process—After Reading

Answer each question in complete sentences.

1. What are the three steps in the After Reading stage?

....

....

....

....

....

2. What is one reason you might decide to reread something?

....

....

....

....

....

NAME

The Reading Process—After Reading

Circle the best answer for each question.

1. Which of these is a step in the After Reading stage of the reading process?

    a. Set a purpose

    b. Plan

    c. Remember

    d. Preview

2. Which is a good question to ask yourself after you've finished reading?

    a. "Did I meet my reading purpose?"

    b. "Did I learn everything I wanted to learn?"

    c. "Did anything confuse me?"

    d. All of the above

3. Which is true about rereading?

    a. Rereading wastes time.

    b. Even good readers need to reread.

    c. There is only one reason to reread.

    d. Most readers learn everything in one reading.

NAME ....

Basic Reading Skills—Part I

Answer each question in complete sentences.

1. What is predicting?

....

....

....

....

....

2. How do you make an inference?

....

....

....

....

....

NAME ....

Basic Reading Skills—Part I

Circle the best answer for each question.

1. What do you do when you predict?

    a. You compare two things.

    b. You make a guess about what will come next.

    c. You tell an idea in your own words.

    d. You explain why something happened.

2. What two things help you make an inference?

    a. What a word means and how you spell it

    b. What happens to you and what happens to your friends

    c. What you already know and what you learn from reading

    d. What you hope will happen and your feelings

3. What can you make inferences about when you read a story?

    a. What a character is like

    b. What is happening

    c. What a sentence means

    d. All of the above

NAME

Basic Reading Skills—Part II

Answer each question in complete sentences.

1. What do you do when you compare and contrast two things?

....

....

....

....

....

2. What do you do when you evaluate something?

....

....

....

....

....

....

NAME

Basic Reading Skills—Part II

Circle the best answer for each question.

1. What do you do when you draw a conclusion?

    a. You predict what will happen next.

    b. You make a picture of a scene in the book.

    c. You put together different bits of information.

    d. You choose a reading strategy.

2. What is a good reading tool to use when you compare and contrast?

    a. Venn Diagram

    b. Story String

    c. K-W-L Chart

    d. Storyboard

3. What do you do when you evaluate a book you just read?

    a. You write a story about it and give it to your friends.

    b. You tell your opinion of whether it is good or bad.

    c. You reread your favorite parts.

    d. You tell a friend what it is about.

Being an Active Reader

Answer each question in complete sentences.

1. What are three ways an active reader may take notes?

....

....

....

....

....

2. Where are three places you can write notes when reading?

....

....

....

....

....

NAME ....

Being an Active Reader

Circle the best answer for each question.

1. What should active readers NOT do as they read?

    a. Keep their minds busy.

    b. Ask questions.

    c. Pass their eyes over the words quickly.

    d. Create pictures in their head.

2. How do you mark key words?

    a. Underline them.

    b. Circle them.

    c. Highlight them.

    d. All of the above

3. When you write notes in a notebook, remember to _____.

    a. use lots of big words and hard sentences

    b. write down the title and the page number

    c. list all the words you don't know

    d. write quickly

NAME ....

Ways to Be a Good Reader

Answer each question in complete sentences.

1. What is the best thing you can do to become a better reader?

....

....

....

....

....

2. What are two things to do when previewing a book?

....

....

....

....

Ways to Be a Good Reader

Circle the best answer for each question.

1. What should a good reading place have?

 a. Good light

 b. Peace and quiet

 c. A comfortable chair

 d. All of the above

2. What should you do when you preview a book?

 a. Look up all the words you don't know.

 b. Look at the first page or two.

 c. Write down all your questions and ideas.

 d. Read the last few pages very slowly.

3. Which is a good tip for finding a book you will like?

 a. Write down your reading plan.

 b. Go through the steps of the reading process.

 c. Ask a librarian or your teacher for ideas.

 d. Reread the parts that confused you.

How to Read Aloud

Answer each question in complete sentences.

1. What are two ways to read smoothly?

....

....

....

....

....

2. What is the best way to prepare for reading aloud?

....

....

....

....

....

NAME

How to Read Aloud

Circle the best answer for each question.

1. To read accurately, what should you do?

    a. Read very slowly.

    b. Use capital letters and periods.

    c. Pronounce each word carefully.

    d. None of the above

2. What should you do to read smoothly?

    a. Think how words go together in groups.

    b. Read without saying "ah" or "um."

    c. Go faster or slower as needed.

    d. All of the above

3. How can you read aloud in an interesting way?

    a. Read softly all of the time.

    b. Do not look at your audience.

    c. Always sound sad.

    d. Change the tone and pitch of your voice.

NAME

Understanding Letters and Sounds

Answer each question in complete sentences.

1. What is a syllable?

....

....

....

....

....

2. How do you figure out a big word you've never seen before?

....

....

....

....

....

NAME ....

Understanding Letters and Sounds

Circle the best answer for each question.

1. Which word shows one way to spell the *f* sound?

   a. *Phone*

   b. *Far*

   c. *Rough*

   d. All of the above

2. What is a syllable?

   a. Part of a word with a vowel sound

   b. The number of consonants in a word

   c. The **long *a*** sound in a word

   d. A group of three letters

3. Which of the following is NOT a way to figure out the meaning of a big word?

   a. Make up a definition.

   b. Look for parts you know.

   c. Look for little words and sounds

   d. Try to sound it out.

NAME

Understanding Words and Word Parts

Answer each question in complete sentences.

1. What is the difference between a prefix and a suffix?

....

....

....

....

....

2. Tell what a homophone is. Give an example.

....

....

....

....

....

NAME

Understanding Words and Word Parts

Circle the best answer for each question.

1. Which is true of a suffix?

   a. It comes at the beginning of a word.

   b. It comes at the end of a word.

   c. It is a root.

   d. It comes in the middle of a word.

2. Which word has a prefix that means "not"?

   a. *Incorrect*

   b. *Nonsense*

   c. *Disagree*

   d. All of the above

3. Which pair of words are homophones?

   a. *Sit, set*

   b. *Below, beneath*

   c. *Their, there*

   d. *Careful, careless*

NAME

Learning New Words and Using a Dictionary

Answer each question in complete sentences.

1. What are two things you can find out about a word by using a dictionary?

....

....

....

....

2. Where are the guide words on a dictionary page? Why are they useful?

....

....

....

....

Learning New Words and Using a Dictionary

Circle the best answer for each question.

1. What can you find out from a dictionary?

   a. How to spell a word

   b. How to split a word into syllables

   c. How to pronounce a word

   d. All of the above

2. Which of these is NOT part of the five-step plan for learning a new word?

   a. Write it down.

   b. Look it up.

   c. Write the definition in your own words.

   d. Memorize the sample sentences in the dictionary.

3. What is the most important thing you can do to improve your vocabulary?

   a. Know all the parts of speech.

   b. Read a lot.

   c. Listen to friends when they talk.

   d. Write long sentences.

NAME

Context Clues and Vocabulary Questions

Answer each question in complete sentences.

1. When you use a context clue, what are you doing?

....

....

....

....

....

2. What is the difference between a synonym and an antonym?

....

....

....

....

....

Context Clues and Vocabulary Questions

Circle the best answer for each question.

1. What is a word's context?

    a. The dictionary definition

    b. The words, phrases, and sentences around it

    c. The author's purpose

    d. All of the above

2. What is a synonym for *big*?

    a. *Large*

    b. *Small*

    c. *Castle*

    d. *Bigger*

3. What should you do to answer a definition question on a test?

    a. Read the question 10–12 times.

    b. Put the answer choices in alphabetical order.

    c. Look for prefixes and suffixes you might know.

    d. Choose the answer with the shortest words.

Understanding Paragraphs

Answer each question in complete sentences.

1. What is a paragraph?

....

....

....

....

....

2. What does a topic sentence tell you?

....

....

....

....

....

NAME

Understanding Paragraphs

Circle the best answer for each question.

1. Which sentence is true?

    a. Paragraphs are all organized in the same way.

    b. Many paragraphs begin with a topic sentence.

    c. All paragraphs have three sentences.

    d. All of the above

2. A paragraph is indented if _____.

    a. it has lots of details

    b. it is short

    c. the first line starts a few spaces to the right

    d. it has a title or a heading

3. Where should you look to find the subject of a paragraph?

    a. At the title or heading, if there is one

    b. At the first sentence

    c. For any repeated or important words

    d. All of the above

Finding the Main Idea

Answer each question in complete sentences.

1. What is the difference between a paragraph's subject and its main idea?

....

....

....

....

....

2. Where are two places the author often gives the main idea?

....

....

....

....

....

....

Finding the Main Idea

Circle the best answer for each question.

1. What does the main idea of a paragraph tell?

    a. The subject

    b. What the author says about the subject

    c. How you feel about the subject

    d. The most important details

2. How can you find the main idea of a paragraph?

    a. By reading the first sentence.

    b. By reading the last sentence.

    c. By putting together all the details.

    d. All of the above

3. A Main Idea Organizer helps you keep track of _____ .

    a. the subject, the main idea, and the details

    b. what you already know about the subject

    c. your questions about the main idea

    d. the number of words

NAME

Kinds of Paragraphs

Answer each question in complete sentences.

1. Describe two kinds of paragraphs.

....

....

....

....

....

2. What reading tool can you use to keep track of details in a paragraph?

....

....

....

....

....

NAME

Kinds of Paragraphs

Circle the best answer for each question.

1. What kind of paragraph gives an opinion?

    a. Narrative

    b. Persuasive

    c. Expository

    d. Descriptive

2. What is the author of an expository paragraph trying to do?

    a. Make you agree with his or her opinion.

    b. Describe an unusual place.

    c. Give information and explain a topic.

    d. Make a prediction.

3. What should you write in the middle circle of a Web about a paragraph?

    a. The least important detail

    b. The first sentence

    c. Words you don't know

    d. The subject

NAME

How Paragraphs Are Organized—Part I

Answer each question in complete sentences.

1. What are two common ways of organizing a paragraph?

....

....

....

....

....

2. How can a Timeline help you understand a paragraph?

....

....

....

....

....

NAME

How Paragraphs Are Organized—Part I

Circle the best answer for each question.

1. Which of these clues signal time order?

    a. Days of the week

    b. Names of places

    c. Colors and sizes

    d. Short paragraphs

2. For location order, how can writers arrange details?

    a. Left to right

    b. Top to bottom

    c. In a circle

    d. All of the above

3. What is true about paragraphs organized in list order?

    a. They all have numbered lists.

    b. The details may be listed in no clear order.

    c. The most important detail is at the end.

    d. There are no details.

NAME

How Paragraphs Are Organized—Part II

Answer each question in complete sentences.

1. What is the difference between a cause and an effect?

....

....

....

....

....

2. What's a good tool to use to understand a comparison-contrast paragraph?

....

....

....

....

....

How Paragraphs Are Organized—Part II

Circle the best answer for each question.

1. What do cause-effect paragraphs tell?

    a. Where something happened

    b. Why something happened

    c. What date something happened

    d. None of the above

2. What tool is useful to keep track of details in a comparison-contrast paragraph?

    a. Cause-Effect Organizer

    b. Character Map

    c. K-W-L Chart

    d. Venn Diagram

3. What do you do when you contrast two things?

    a. Show how they are alike.

    b. Show how they are different.

    c. State your opinion of them.

    d. Research facts about them.

NAME

Reading an Article

Answer each question in complete sentences.

1. What are two things to look at when you preview an article?

....

....

....

....

....

2. How is the strategy of summarizing useful when you read an article?

....

....

....

....

....

Reading an Article

Circle the best answer for each question.

1. Which of these should you look at when you preview an article?

    a. First and last paragraphs

    b. Words in boldface

    c. Illustrations and photos

    d. All of the above

2. Which strategy do you use when you want to retell the main points of an article?

    a. Skimming

    b. Summarizing

    c. Close Reading

    d. Visualizing and Thinking Aloud

3. Which of these is a good tool for reading an article?

    a. Fiction Organizer

    b. Venn Diagram

    c. 5 W's and H Organizer

    d. Double-entry Journal

NAME

Reading a Biography

Answer each question in complete sentences.

1. What is a biography?

_____

_____

_____

_____

_____

2. Why is a Timeline a good reading tool to use with a biography?

_____

_____

_____

_____

_____

NAME

Reading a Biography

Circle the best answer for each question.

1. Why might you read a biography?

    a. To learn what the person was really like

    b. To take notes

    c. To enjoy the plot and setting

    d. To memorize facts

2. Which of these items is important to preview in a biography?

    a. The front and back covers

    b. The last sentence of every paragraph

    c. The last two chapters

    d. The index

3. Which reading tool helps you keep track of important dates in a person's life?

    a. Cause-Effect Organizer

    b. K-W-L Chart

    c. Venn Diagram

    d. Timeline

Information Books and Encyclopedias

Answer each question in complete sentences.

1. What are two things to look for when you preview an information book?

....

....

....

....

....

2. What is an encyclopedia?

....

....

....

....

....

NAME ....

Information Books and Encyclopedias

Circle the best answer for each question.

1. What should you look for when you preview an information book?

    a. Table of contents

    b. Headings

    c. Pictures

    d. All of the above

2. What tool will help you keep track of facts in an information book?

    a. Fiction Organizer

    b. Character Map

    c. Web Card

    d. Summary Notes

3. What is true about encyclopedias?

    a. They can be books or CDs.

    b. Articles in them tell only opinions, not facts.

    c. The names of the people who write the articles are never given.

    d. They are a kind of fiction writing.

NAME ....

Websites and Graphics

Answer each question in complete sentences.

1. Why do you need a clear purpose when you read a website?

....

....

....

....

....

2. What does a bar graph show?

....

....

....

....

....

50

Websites and Graphics

Circle the best answer for each question.

1. What should you do when you read a website?

    a. Set a clear purpose.

    b. Preview the site.

    c. Use the headings to stay on track.

    d. All of the above

2. What should you do when you take notes about a website?

    a. Look at several web pages before writing anything down.

    b. Skip the graphics and don't take notes on them.

    c. Write down the website address.

    d. All of the above

3. What should you do first when you read a table?

    a. Draw a conclusion about what the table says.

    b. Read the title and the column and row headings.

    c. Write down all the important numbers.

    d. Talk about it with a friend.

NAME ....

Elements of Nonfiction and Textbooks

Answer each question in complete sentences.

1. What is the difference between a fact and an opinion?

....

....

....

....

....

2. When would you use the index of a textbook?

....

....

....

....

....

Elements of Nonfiction and Textbooks

Circle the best answer for each question.

1. Which is true of a line graph?

    a. It is a label on a diagram.

    b. The most important part is a photo.

    c. It shows change over time.

    d. It never has a title.

2. What does a circle graph show?

    a. Steps in a process

    b. Parts of a whole

    c. Important dates

    d. Details about a fact

3. What does a glossary include?

    a. A list of key terms and their definitions

    b. A list of cities and maps

    c. A summary of main ideas

    d. Review questions

NAME

Reading Social Studies

Answer each question in complete sentences.

1. What are two things to preview in a social studies textbook?

....

....

....

....

....

2. Explain why using graphic organizers is a good strategy for reading social studies.

....

....

....

....

....

Reading Social Studies

Circle the best answer for each question.

1. Which reading strategy helps you keep track of and remember key details?

    a. Using your own words

    b. Using graphic organizers

    c. Predicting

    d. Previewing

2. What does the "L" in a K-W-L Chart stand for?

    a. Listen

    b. Last

    c. Learned

    d. Liked

3. What do the headings in a social studies chapter tell you?

    a. The author's opinion

    b. Where the maps are

    c. What vocabulary words mean

    d. What smaller topics are covered

NAME

Reading Science

Answer each question in complete sentences.

1. What is a good strategy for reading a science chapter? Explain why.

....

....

....

....

....

2. How do you make a personal connection to science?

....

....

....

....

....

Reading Science

Circle the best answer for each question.

1. What is a good way to preview a science chapter?

    a. Look at headings, previews, and photos.

    b. Do an experiment.

    c. Read each sentence slowly.

    d. Connect the facts to your own life.

2. Which of these is a good note-taking tool to use for reading science?

    a. Double-entry Journal

    b. Storyboard

    c. Process Notes

    d. Character Map

3. When you read about causes and effects, what are you learning?

    a. Why something happened

    b. What year something was started

    c. The parts of a diagram

    d. Key terms

NAME

Reading Math

Answer each question in complete sentences.

1. What strategy is useful for reading a math textbook?

....

....

....

....

2. What are two things to look at when you preview a math textbook?

....

....

....

....

NAME

Reading Math

Circle the best answer for each question.

1. What should you look at when you preview a chapter in a math textbook?

    a. Sample problems and their solutions

    b. The first word in each paragraph

    c. The index

    d. None of the above

2. What do you do when you use the strategy of visualizing and thinking aloud?

    a. Read only the most important words.

    b. Guess which answers are correct.

    c. Draw a picture and think through your ideas.

    d. Make a prediction and tell everyone about it.

3. Why should you make Summary Notes?

    a. To remember the answers to the sample problems

    b. To plan what reading strategy to use

    c. To help you think about and remember key ideas

    d. To memorize all the practice problems

NAME ....

Word Problems and Questions

Answer each question in complete sentences.

1. What are the four steps to follow when solving word problems?

....

....

....

....

....

2. What two things do you need to put together to answer a critical thinking question?

....

....

....

....

....

NAME

Word Problems and Questions

Circle the best answer for each question.

1. What should you look for when you preview a math word problem?

    a. The main question and key facts

    b. The first and last words

    c. Names of people and places

    d. All of the above

2. Which is NOT a step in the four-step plan for solving word problems?

    a. Read

    b. Solve

    c. React

    d. Check

3. What is true about fact questions?

    a. They ask for your opinions.

    b. The answers will be "right there" in the reading.

    c. They have no key words and you have to make an inference.

    d. You should not preview them.

NAME ....

Reading a Folktale

Answer each question in complete sentences.

1. What is a folktale?

....

....

....

....

....

2. What reading strategy can help you remember the main events in a folktale?

....

....

....

....

....

Reading a Folktale

Circle the best answer for each question.

1. What is true about folktales?

    a. They are one of the oldest kinds of stories.

    b. They are about real people and events.

    c. They are always long.

    d. All of the above

2. What is a good purpose question to use when you read a folktale?

    a. Who wrote the folktale?

    b. When was the folktale written?

    c. What is the main lesson I will learn?

    d. Do I know anybody who is like the main character?

3. What reading tool helps you see how one event leads to the next in a folktale?

    a. Double-entry Journal

    b. Setting Chart

    c. Web

    d. Story String

NAME

Reading a Novel

Answer each question in complete sentences.

1. What is a good reading strategy to use with a novel? Why?

....

....

....

....

....

2. What reading tool can help you keep track of what a character is like?

....

....

....

....

....

Reading a Novel

Circle the best answer for each question.

1. Which would NOT make a good purpose question for reading a novel?

   a. What happens?

   b. Who wrote it?

   c. Who are the main characters?

   d. Where and when does it take place?

2. What does a Fiction Organizer include?

   a. Details about the author's life

   b. A picture of the main character and setting

   c. Details about the characters, plot, and setting

   d. All of the above

3. What reading strategy works well when you read a novel?

   a. Using graphic organizers

   b. Using your own words

   c. Skimming

   d. Visualizing and thinking aloud

NAME

Plot, Dialogue, and Theme

Answer each question in complete sentences.

1. What do you find out in the beginning of most stories?

....

....

....

....

....

2. What is the theme of a story?

....

....

....

....

....

Plot, Dialogue, and Theme

Circle the best answer for each question.

1. What is the climax of a plot?

    a. Where you learn about the problem and characters

    b. The part where the problem is about to be solved

    c. The beginning

    d. The end

2. What is true about dialogue in a story?

    a. Most dialogue is put inside quotation marks.

    b. Speech tags tell who says what.

    c. Dialogue is the talking that characters do.

    d. All of the above

3. What is the theme of a story?

    a. The subject

    b. The character's problem

    c. The way the problem is solved

    d. The author's main point about life

NAME

Characters and Setting

Answer each question in complete sentences.

1. What is a good reading tool to use to track the changes a character goes through?

....

....

....

....

2. What is the setting of a story?

....

....

....

....

Characters and Setting

Circle the best answer for each question.

1. What does a Character Change Chart show?

    a. The names of minor and major characters

    b. The character in the beginning, middle, and end

    c. Your opinion of a character

    d. All of the above

2. Where can you find clues about what characters are like?

    a. The description of the setting

    b. The last sentence on each page

    c. What they say and what they do

    d. All of the above

3. What does a Setting Chart show?

    a. The author's style

    b. Clues about time and about place

    c. Pictures at the beginning and end

    d. What you think the theme is

NAME

Elements of Literature

Answer each question in complete sentences.

1. What is a story's mood?

....

....

....

....

....

2. What are two different kinds of narrators?

....

....

....

....

....

NAME

Elements of Literature

Circle the best answer for each question.

1. What do you call the feeling that a story gives you?

    a. Onomatopoeia

    b. Personification

    c. Imagery

    d. Mood

2. Which of these sentences shows alliteration?

    a. The bed was on a sled.

    b. Tim tells time too.

    c. The cow said, "Moo."

    d. The puppy ran after the car.

3. What is true about a story with a third-person narrator?

    a. It is told by someone who is not in the story.

    b. It uses words such as *I, my,* and *me.*

    c. It is told by the main character in the story.

    d. It has no theme.

NAME ....

Reading a Poem

Answer each question in complete sentences.

1. What is a good reading strategy to use when you read a poem? Why?

....

....

....

....

....

2. What are two things to look for when you preview a poem?

....

....

....

....

....

NAME

Reading a Poem

Circle the best answer for each question.

1. Which reading tool helps you put a poem into your own words?

    a. Web

    b. Plot Diagram

    c. Double-entry Journal

    d. Character Map

2. What should you do when reading a poem?

    a. Preview the first and last lines.

    b. Try to read the poem three times.

    c. Connect the poem to your own life.

    d. All of the above

3. What makes poems different from novels and information books?

    a. Most poems are longer and use difficult words.

    b. Many poems have interesting shapes and sounds.

    c. Poems are nonfiction.

    d. Poems have no meaning.

NAME ....

Reading a Test and Test Questions

Answer each question in complete sentences.

1. What reading strategy should you use to find key words on a test?

....

....

....

....

....

2. How is a critical thinking question different from a fact question?

....

....

....

....

....

Reading a Test and Test Questions

Circle the best answer for each question.

1. Why is skimming a good strategy to use when you read a test?

    a. It helps you understand every word.

    b. It helps you connect to what you read.

    c. It helps you find key words and phrases quickly.

    d. All of the above

2. What should you look at when you preview a test?

    a. You should not preview a test.

    b. Words you don't know

    c. The directions and kinds of questions

    d. The last sentence on each page

3. What do you put together to answer a critical thinking question?

    a. Information from the reading and what you already know

    b. What your teacher says and what your classmates say

    c. Words in the directions and words in the questions

    d. Facts from the first and last paragraphs

NAME

Reading Tests and Language Tests

Answer each question in complete sentences.

1. How can you find the answer to a fact question about a reading passage?

....

....

....

....

....

2. What are two things you should do when you finish a test?

....

....

....

....

....

Reading Tests and Language Tests

Circle the best answer for each question.

1. What should you NOT do when you're previewing a passage on a test?

    a. Look at the title.

    b. Look for repeated words.

    c. Make a list of words you're not sure how to spell.

    d. Read the first and last sentence of each paragraph.

2. After you find the key words in a fact question, what should you do?

    a. Look for those same key words in the reading passage.

    b. Set your purpose.

    c. Decide if the passage is hard or easy.

    d. List three ways to connect the topic to your own life.

3. What should you do after you've read and understood the question?

    a. Read through each answer choice carefully.

    b. Rule out answers that you think are wrong.

    c. Think through the question again and choose the best answer.

    d. All of the above

NAME

Writing Tests and Math Tests

Answer each question in complete sentences.

1. What are two things you should check when you finish your writing?

....

....

....

....

....

2. What do the key words in a math problem tell you?

....

....

....

....

....

Writing Tests and Math Tests

Circle the best answer for each question.

1. What should you do before you start to write your answer on a writing test?

    a. Preview the test.

    b. Read the directions carefully.

    c. Use an organizer to help you plan what to write.

    d. All of the above

2. Which of these should you NOT do when you check your writing?

    a. Check your spelling.

    b. Be sure you stayed on the topic.

    c. Make sure each paragraph has three sentences.

    d. Indent each new paragraph.

3. What reading strategy is useful for answering math problems?

    a. Using graphic organizers

    b. Summarizing

    c. Visualizing and thinking aloud

    d. Skimming

Assessment Rubrics

The following pages offer four different rubrics that outline the reading skills and strategies discussed in the *Reader's Handbook*. This program offers a Quick Assess checklist and formal test for each lesson. However, not all assessment needs to come from a formal test.

Observing how students use skills and strategies is another good way of assessing their overall knowledge. These rubrics are designed for use in the classroom as a quick method of taking an informal assessment on each student. You can make notes as you walk around the classroom and observe them at work. You can work with students in small groups or on an individual basis.

Keep the rubrics on each child in a folder so you can track individual growth. The rubrics help you to identify areas of proficiency, as well as areas where a student is struggling. You can take an assessment on each child at the beginning, middle, and end of the school year. Or you can use these monthly or quarterly. They maybe helpful before a grading period or before parent conferences take place. Students may even benefit from seeing them as well.

These rubrics are aligned with the skills and strategies presented in the *Reader's Handbook*. The topics covered in the rubrics are:

■ **The Reading Process**
■ **Reading Strategies**
■ **Fluency**
■ **Reading Skills**

NAME .... DATE ....

The Reading Process

	Emerging				Proficient

Before Reading

Set a Purpose
  Form reading purpose questions.
  Define reason for reading.
  Recognize different reasons for reading.

Preview
  Make appropriate book choices.
  Previews different parts of a reading.

Plan
  Form a plan for reading.
  Choose an appropriate strategy.
  Choose appropriate reading tools.

During Reading

Read with a Purpose
  Demonstrate active reading skills.
  Focus on reading purpose questions.

Connect
  Connect reading to personal experiences.
  Relate story to what is already known.

After Reading

Pause and Reflect
  Refer back to purpose questions.
  Reflect on the reading.

Reread
  Choose appropriate part(s) to reread.
  Demonstrate reasons to reread.

Remember
  Find a way to use information.
  Write or explain in own words.

Scale: Emerging → Proficient (1 2 3 4 5)

Additional Comments:

....

....

....

NAME .... DATE ....

Reading Strategies

	Emerging			Proficient	
	1	2	3	4	5

Note-taking
Take notes on key words or ideas.
Keep track of important details.
Focus notes on topic.
Study notes to remember information.

Skimming
Get a quick idea of information included.
Skim for general ideas.
Skim for details.
Skim for key words on tests.

Summarizing
Summarize main ideas and events.
Summarize details and facts.
Summarize fiction.
Summarize nonfiction.

Using Graphic Organizers
Organize information appropriately.
Highlight key details in fiction.
Apply a graphic organizer to nonfiction.
Use a variety of graphic organizers.

Using Your Own Words
Identify general topic.
Read for key details.
Explain the overall meaning.

Visualizing and Thinking Aloud
Discover the facts needed.
Sketch key information.
Talk through a problem and how to
    answer it.

Additional Comments:

....

....

NAME .... DATE ....

Fluency

	Emerging				Proficient
	1	2	3	4	5

Preparation

Research unknown words. ☐ ☐ ☐ ☐ ☐

Practice reading ahead of time. ☐ ☐ ☐ ☐ ☐

Clear and Accurate

Read without skipping or stumbling over words. ☐ ☐ ☐ ☐ ☐

Read loudly and clearly. ☐ ☐ ☐ ☐ ☐

Pronounce words carefully. ☐ ☐ ☐ ☐ ☐

Decode words accurately. ☐ ☐ ☐ ☐ ☐

Read Smoothly

Read with a rhythm. ☐ ☐ ☐ ☐ ☐

Vary speed when appropriate. ☐ ☐ ☐ ☐ ☐

Read without adding "ah" and "um." ☐ ☐ ☐ ☐ ☐

Reflect punctuation in voice. ☐ ☐ ☐ ☐ ☐

Group words and phrases together. ☐ ☐ ☐ ☐ ☐

Adds Expression

Reflect feeling of reading. ☐ ☐ ☐ ☐ ☐

Vary tone and pitch of voice. ☐ ☐ ☐ ☐ ☐

Stress key words. ☐ ☐ ☐ ☐ ☐

Make eye contact. ☐ ☐ ☐ ☐ ☐

Additional Comments:

....

....

....

....

NAME ....   DATE ....

Reading Skills

	Emerging			Proficient	
	1	2	3	4	5

Active Reading Skills

	1	2	3	4	5
Predict.	☐	☐	☐	☐	☐
Make inferences.	☐	☐	☐	☐	☐
Draw conclusions.	☐	☐	☐	☐	☐
Compare and contrast.	☐	☐	☐	☐	☐
Evaluate.	☐	☐	☐	☐	☐
Mark and take notes.	☐	☐	☐	☐	☐

Vocabulary

	1	2	3	4	5
Break words into parts.	☐	☐	☐	☐	☐
Understand prefixes.	☐	☐	☐	☐	☐
Understand suffixes.	☐	☐	☐	☐	☐
Understand roots.	☐	☐	☐	☐	☐
Use of a dictionary.	☐	☐	☐	☐	☐

Comprehension Skills

	1	2	3	4	5
Use context clues.	☐	☐	☐	☐	☐
Recognize subject of paragraph.	☐	☐	☐	☐	☐
Find main idea.	☐	☐	☐	☐	☐

Genres

	1	2	3	4	5
Understand characteristics of genre.	☐	☐	☐	☐	☐
Identify reading strategy to use with each genre.	☐	☐	☐	☐	☐
Use appropriate reading tools for genre.	☐	☐	☐	☐	☐

Additional Comments:

....

....

....

....

Answer Key

Introduction

Short-answer Test

1. *Answers may include two of the following*: you read for fun, it gives you information, and it changes you.

2. Reading is thinking. It is a skill, a tool, and a process.

Multiple-choice Test

1. a   2. c   3. b

The Reading Process—Before Reading

Short-answer Test

1. You set a reading purpose because you read for a reason.

2. *Answers may include two of the following*: the title, the first sentence, the pictures, and the ending.

Multiple-choice Test

1. c   2. d   3. a

The Reading Process—During Reading

Short-answer Test

1. Ask yourself, "What am I trying to learn here?"

2. You connect to a reading by asking yourself questions about how the reading relates to your life.

Multiple-choice Test

1. c   2. d   3. a

The Reading Process—After Reading

Short-answer Test

1. The three steps are Pause and Reflect, Reread, and Remember.

2. *Answers may include*: to learn more details, to look again at a part that seemed confusing, and to enjoy again.

Multiple-choice Test

1. c   2. d   3. b

Basic Reading Skills—Part I

Short-answer Test

1. Predicting is when you use what you know to make a guess at what will come next.

2. You make an inference by putting together what you know and what you learn from the reading.

Multiple-choice Test

1. b   2. c   3. d

Basic Reading Skills—Part II

Short-answer Test

1. You think about how they are alike and how they are different.

2. You give your opinion about whether something is good or bad and whether you like it or not.

Multiple-choice Test

1. c   2. a   3. b

Being an Active Reader

Short-answer Test

1. *Answers may include*: mark or highlight key words, react to the words, ask questions, create pictures, make things clear, and predict.

2. Three places to write notes are on sticky notes, on the page, and in a notebook.

Multiple-choice Test

1. c   2. d   3. b

Ways to Be a Good Reader

Short-answer Test

1. You can find time to read for fun every day.

2. *Answers may include*: look at the front and back cover, look at the first page or two, look at the table of contents, and flip through the pages.

Multiple-choice Test

1. d   2. b   3. c

How to Read Aloud

Short-answer Test

1. *Answers may include*: to read with a rhythm, go faster or slower as needed, don't say "ah" or "um," and to think about how words go together in groups.

2. The best way to prepare for reading aloud is to practice.

Multiple-choice Test

1. c   **2.** d   **3.** d

Understanding Letters and Sounds

Short-answer Test

1. A syllable is each part of a word with a vowel sound.

2. Look for little words and sounds that you know. Then put them together to make parts that you do know. Last, put everything together to figure out the meaning.

Multiple-choice Test

1. d   **2.** a   **3.** a

Understanding Words and Word Parts

Short-answer Test

1. A prefix is a word part that is added to the beginning of the word, and a suffix is added to the end of a word.

2. Homophones are words that sound exactly alike, but they have a different spelling and a different meaning. Examples will vary, such as: *ant / aunt*; *here / hear*, and so on.

Multiple-choice Test

1. b   **2.** d   **3.** c

Learning New Words and Using a Dictionary

Short-answer Test

1. *Answers may include*: what a word means, how to spell a word, how to pronounce a word, and how to split a word into syllables.

2. Guide words are shown at the top of the page. They tell you what the first and last words on that page are.

Multiple-choice Test

1. d   **2.** d   **3.** b

Context Clues and Vocabulary Questions

Short-answer Test

1. You are figuring out what a word means from the words, phrases, and sentences around the word.

2. Synonyms mean the same thing, and antonyms mean the opposite of each other.

Multiple-choice Test

1. b   **2.** a   **3.** c

Understanding Paragraphs

Short-answer Test

1. A paragraph is a group of several sentences about the same subject.

2. A topic sentence tells what the paragraph is about and what the main point is.

Multiple-choice Test

1. b   **2.** c   **3.** d

Finding the Main Idea

Short-answer Test

1. The subject is what the paragraph is about, and the main idea is what the author says about the subject.

2. The author often gives the main idea in the first or last sentence.

Multiple-choice Test

1. b   **2.** d   **3.** a

Kinds of Paragraphs

Short-answer Test

1. *Answers may include*: A narrative paragraph tells a story; a descriptive paragraph describes; a persuasive paragraph gives an opinion; and an expository paragraph gives information.

2. A good reading tool to help keep track of detail in a paragraph is a Web or Summary Notes.

Multiple-choice Test

1. b   **2.** c   **3.** d

How Paragraphs Are Organized—Part I

Short-answer Test

1. *Answers may include*: time order, location order, comparison-contrast order, list order, and cause-effect order.

2. A Timeline helps you understand the order of events in a paragraph.

Multiple-choice Test

1. a   **2.** d   **3.** b

How Paragraphs Are Organized—Part II

Short-answer Test

1. The cause is what makes something happen, and the effect is what happens.

2. A good tool to use for comparing is a Venn Diagram.

Multiple-choice Test

1. b   **2.** d   **3.** b

Reading an Article

Short-answer Test

1. *Answers may include*: the title and headings, first and last paragraphs, illustrations and photos, and words in boldface.
2. Summarizing is useful because it helps you find or focus on the important details.

Multiple-choice Test

1. d   **2.** b   **3.** c

Reading a Biography

Short-answer Test

1. A biography is the true story of someone's life.
2. A Timeline is an easy way to keep track of the key dates and events.

Multiple-choice Test

1. a   **2.** a   **3.** d

Information Books and Encyclopedias

Short-answer Test

1. *Answers my include*: table of contents, pictures, headings, and the index.
2. An encyclopedia is a collection of articles, in alphabetical order, on all types of topics.

Multiple-choice Test

1. d   **2.** d   **3.** a

Websites and Graphics

Short-answer Test

1. Having a clear purpose makes it easier to find the information you need.

2. A bar graph shows how two or more things compare at one point in time.

Multiple-choice Test

1. d   **2.** c   **3.** b

Elements of Nonfiction and Textbooks

Short-answer Test

1. A fact is something that can be proved, and an opinion is someone's personal belief.

2. You use an index when you want to find the page numbers for specific information on a topic in a book.

Multiple-choice Test

1. c   **2.** b   **3.** a

Reading Social Studies

Short-answer Test

1. *Answers may include*: title and headings; pictures, maps, charts, and diagrams; names, dates, and words in boldface; and previews, summaries, and questions.

2. Using graphic organizers is a good strategy because it helps you keep track of key details. Different organizers can help you understand and remember what you've read.

Multiple-choice Test

1. b   **2.** c   **3.** d

Reading Science

Short-answer Test

1. A good strategy is note-taking. Writing notes helps you understand and remember what you have read.

2. You try to see how it fits with your life and ask what does the information have to do with you.

Multiple-choice Test

1. a **2.** c **3.** a

Reading Math

Short-answer Test

1. A useful strategy for reading math is visualizing and thinking aloud.

2. *Answers may include*: lesson title and headings; sample problems and their solutions; practice problems; and boxed items and questions.

Multiple-choice Test

1. a **2.** c **3.** c

Word Problems and Questions

Short-answer Test

1. The four steps to follow are read, plan, solve, and check.

2. You need to put together the details from the text with what you already know.

Multiple-choice Test

1. a **2.** c **3.** b

Reading a Folktale

Short-answer Test

1. A folktale is a made-up story that teaches an important lesson about life.

2. A reading strategy to help you remember the main events in a folktale is summarizing.

Multiple-choice Test

1. a   **2.** c   **3.** d

Reading a Novel

Short-answer Test

1. A good reading strategy is using graphic organizers because it helps you see what is important and how the parts fit together.

2. A Character Map will help you keep track of what a character is like.

Multiple-choice Test

1. b   **2.** c   **3.** a

Plot, Dialogue, and Theme

Short-answer Test

1. In the beginning of a story you find out about the characters and what the main problem is.

2. The theme of a story is the main idea about life that the author wants to get across in a story.

Multiple-choice Test

1. b   **2.** d   **3.** d

Characters and Setting

Short-answer Test

1. A good reading tool to use to keep track of a characters' changes is a Character Change Chart.

2. The setting of a story is where and when it takes place.

Multiple-choice Test

1. b   **2.** c   **3.** b

Elements of Literature

Short-answer Test

1. A story's mood is the feeling that it gives you.

2. The two kinds of narrators are first-person narrators and third-person narrators.

Multiple-choice Test

1. d   **2.** b   **3.** a

Reading a Poem

Short-answer Test

1. A good reading strategy is using your own words. It makes you think about the poem's meaning.

2. *Answers may include*: title and author, shape of the poem, and first and last lines.

Multiple-choice Test

1. c   **2.** d   **3.** b

Reading a Test and Test Questions

Short-answer Test

1. To find the key words on a test, use the strategy of skimming.

2. For a critical thinking question you need to make inferences to answer it. For a fact question, the answer is "right there" in the text.

Multiple-choice Test

1. c   **2.** c   **3.** a

Reading Tests and Language Tests

Short-answer Test

1. To find the answer to a fact question, return to the reading. Look for key words. The answer will be "right there" in the text.

2. *Answer may include*: look at the easy questions to make sure you marked the right answer, try again to answer the hard questions, make sure you haven't skipped any questions, and make sure the answers are marked clearly.

Multiple-choice Test

1. c   **2.** a   **3.** d

Writing Tests and Math Tests

Short-answer Test

1. *Answers may include*: That everything asked for is included, you stayed on topic, you indented, and used correct spelling and complete sentences.

2. The key words tell you what information you need to solve the math problem.

Multiple-choice Test

1. d   **2.** c   **3.** c